PRIVATE EYE's
Colemanballs
3

A selection of quotes, most
of which originally appeared in
PRIVATE EYE's 'Colemanballs'
column.
Once again, our thanks
to the readers who
sent us their
contrib

D0294292

If you enjoyed this book,
the best-selling first

Colemanballs

is still available, as is

Colemanballs 2

COLEMANBALLS TOP TEN

Place	Name	Entries
1	David Coleman	44
2	Ted Lowe	34
3	Murray Walker	23
4	Peter Jones	17
5	Harry Carpenter	16
6	Bryon Butler	15
7	Trevor Bailey	14
	Simon Bates	14
9	Brian Moore	13
	Ron Pickering	13
	Peter Powell	13

Figures compiled by the Neasden Institute of Statistics. E&OE

PRIVATE EYE's
Colemanballs
3

Compiled and edited by
Barry Fantoni

Illustrated by Larry

PRIVATE EYE/ANDRÉ DEUTSCH

Published in Great Britain 1986 by
Private Eye Productions Limited,
6 Carlisle Street, London W1

In association with André Deutsch Limited
105-106 Great Russell Street, London WC1

ⓒ Pressdram Limited

9 8 7 6 5 4 3 2 1

ISBN 233 97985 9

Typeset by JH Graphics Ltd, Reading

Printed in Great Britain by
Richard Clay (The Chaucer Press) Ltd
Bungay, Suffolk

Athletics

Britain's last gold medal was a bronze in 1952 in
Helsinki.

NIGEL STARMER-SMITH

Steve Ovett, Sebastian Coe, Steve Cram – the vanguard of our cream.

RON PICKERING

The Americans sowed the seed, and now they have reaped the whirlwind.

SEBASTIAN COE

The Republic of China – back in the Olympic Games for the first time.

DAVID COLEMAN

And Britain defeats the rest of the world to pick up the bronze medal.

ANON

He's been breaking Olympic records like ninepins.

DESMOND LYNAM

That's the fastest time ever run – but it's not as fast as the world record.

DAVID COLEMAN

I'm absolutely thrilled and over the world about it.

TESSA SANDERSON

He is accelerating all the time. That last lap was run in 64 seconds and the one before that in 62 seconds.

DAVID COLEMAN

Cram nailed his colours to the mast and threw down the Great Pretender.

RON PICKERING

This is a young man who is only 25, and you have to say, he has answered every question that has ever been asked.

DAVID COLEMAN

Mary Decker Slaney, the world's greatest front runner . . . I shouldn't be surprised to see her at the front.

RON PICKERING

A truly international field, no Britons involved.

DAVID COLEMAN

The Americans' heads are on their chins a little bit at the moment.

RON PICKERING

She hasn't run faster than herself before.

ZOLA BUDD

Born in America, John returned to his native Japan.

MIKE GRATTON

Ingrid Kristiansen, then, has smashed the world record, running the 5,000 metres in 14 minutes 58.89 seconds. Truly amazing. Incidentally, this is a personal best for Ingrid Kristiansen.

DAVID COLEMAN

The Kenyans haven't done much in the last two games – in fact they haven't competed since 1972.

BRENDAN FOSTER

We estimate, and this isn't an estimation, that Greta Waitz is 80 seconds behind.

DAVID COLEMAN

And there's no 'I love you' message, because Steve Ovett has married the girl.

DAVID COLEMAN

The games have been decimated. If you take away the Eastern bloc, you take away fifty percent of the medals.

RON PICKERING

And there you see Seb Coe preparing for our first sight of him.

JIM ROSENTHAL

Boxing

He looks up at him through blood-smeared lips.

HARRY CARPENTER

Marvellous oriental pace he's got – Just like a
Buddhist statue.

HARRY CARPENTER

It's not one of Bruno's fastest wins ... but it's one of
them.

HARRY CARPENTER

I've only seen Errol Christie fight once before and
that was the best I've ever seen him fight.

MARK KAYLOR

This boxer doing what's expected of him – bleeding from the nose.

HARRY CARPENTER

He's got a cut on his left eye ... it's just below his eyebrow.

HARRY CARPENTER

I had Bernard Taylor five rounds ahead going into the fifth round.

ALAN MINTER

Pedroza – the crown on his head hanging by a thread.

HARRY CARPENTER

Cricket

In the rear, the small diminutive figure of Shoaif Mohammed, who can't be much taller or shorter than he is.

HENRY BLOFELD

His throw went absolutely nowhere near where it was going.

RICHIE BENAUD

That was a tremendous six: the ball was still in the air as it went over the boundary.

FRED TRUEMAN

Alderman knows that he is either going to get a wicket – or he isn't.

STEVE BRENKLEY

. . . and Marshall throws his head to his hands!

CHRISTOPHER MARTIN-JENKINS

He's no mean slouch as a bowler.

MIKE DENNESS

The pattern of the match is certainly swaying towards Kent.

TOM GRAVENEY

It's a catch he would have caught ninety-nine times out of a thousand.

HENRY BLOFELD

Even Downton couldn't get down high enough for that.

RICHIE BENAUD

There are good one-day players; there are good Test players – and vice versa . . .

T. E. BAILEY

That black cloud is coming from the direction the wind is blowing . . . Now the wind is coming from where the black cloud is.

RAY ILLINGWORTH

And he's got the guts to score runs when the crunch is down.

JOHN MURRAY

The Sri Lankan team have lost their heads – literally.
GAMINE GOONASENA

For any budding cricketers listening do you have any superstitious routines before an innings, like putting one pad on first, then the other one?

TONY LEWIS

We owe some gratitude to Gatting and Lamb, who breathed some life into a corpse which had nearly expired.

TREVOR BAILEY

It was a good tour to break my teeth in.

BERNARD THOMAS

That slow motion replay doesn't show how fast the ball was travelling.

RICHIE BENAUD

That's what cricket is all about – two batsmen pitting their wits against one another.

FRED TRUEMAN

I don't think he expected it, and that's what caught him unawares.

TREVOR BAILEY

The Queen's Park Oval – exactly as its name suggests – absolutely round.

TONY COZIER

Well, everyone is enjoying this except Vic Marks, and I think he's enjoying himself.

DON MOSEY

Cycling

Cycling's a good thing for the youngsters, because it keeps them off the streets.

DAVID BEAN

Darts

He's ranked number three in Britain, number four in the world. You can't get any higher!

JOHN LOWE

Football

Fifty-two thousand people here at Maine Road tonight, but my goodness me, it seems like fifty thousand . . .

BRYON BUTLER

In the Scottish Cup you only get one crack at the cherry against Rangers or Celtic.

TOM FERRIE

And now the formalities are over, we'll have the National Anthems.

BRIAN MOORE

Wembley way is beginning to blacken with people in terms of red and blue.

ALAN JACKSON

Plenty of goals in Divisions Three and Four today. Darlington nil, Hereford nil.

COMMENTATOR, RADIO 2

Anything from 1-nil to 2-nil would be a nice result.

BOBBY ROBSON

That now means that from the British point of view, Anderlecht lead by three goals to two.

BRYON BUTLER

There were two second division matches last night, both in the second division . . .

DOMINIC ALLEN

The whole team stopped as one man, but Arkwright in particular.

BRIAN MOORE

I don't hold water with that theory.

RON GREENWOOD

I think Charlie George was one of Arsenal's all time great players. A lot of people might not agree with that, but I personally do.

JIMMY GREAVES

They have more ability in the middle of the field in terms of ability.

JIMMY ARMFIELD

It's now 4–3 to Oldham. The goals are going in like dominoes.

SPORTS PRESENTER, PICCADILLY RADIO

The margin is very marginal.

BOBBY ROBSON

And Watford acknowledge the support of the crowd, indeed of the crowd that supported them.

BARRY DAVIES

At least it was a victory and at least we won.

BOBBY MOORE

And Sheffield Wednesday the winners by two goals to nil, leaving the Anfield crowd brainwashed.

STUART HALL

Despite the rain, it's still raining here at Old Trafford.

JIMMY HILL

There are still hundreds of question marks to be answered.

JIMMY ARMFIELD

Yes, Woodcock would have scored but his shot was just too perfect.

RON ATKINSON

It slid away from his left boot which was poised with the trigger cocked.

BARRY DAVIES

We have been saying this, both pre-season and before the season started.

LEN ASHURST

But, as you know, the result for City is not as bad as it sounds on paper.

STEVE McILLWENN

We go into the second half with United 1–0 up, so the game is perfectly balanced.

PETER JONES

Manchester United have got the bull between the horns now.

BILLY MACNEIL

I'll never play at Wembley again, unless I play there again.

KEVIN KEEGAN

Yes, he is not unused to playing mid-field, but at the same time he's not used to playing there, either.

EMLYN HUGHES

The run of the ball is not in our court at the moment.

PHIL NEAL

Well Terry, can you tell us where you are in the
league, how far are you ahead of the second team?

IAN ST JOHN

Runners up at **Wembley** four times – never the bride
always the bridegroom, Leicester.

PETER JONES

Halifax against Spurs – the original David against
Goliath confrontation.

JOHN HELM

That goal surprised most people, least of all myself.

GARTH CROOKS

Well actually we got the winner up there with three minutes to go, but then they equalised.

IAN McNAIL

Ian Rush. Deadly ten times out of ten. But that wasn't one of them.

PETER JONES

He hit the post, and after the game people will say, well he hit the post.

JIMMY GREAVES

I think you and the referee were in a minority of one, Billy.

JIMMY ARMFIELD

Portsmouth are at Huddersfield, which is always away.

JIMMY GREAVES

The red hair of John Brown on the bench there.

ARCHIE McPHERSON

Newport 0, Wrexham 1. Well done the Welsh there!

SPORT ON 2

This is the one-off occasion and you can't get any bigger occasion than that.

BRYAN ROBSON

It was a fair decision, the penalty, even though it was debatable whether it was outside or inside the box.

BOBBY CHARLTON

Believe it or not, goals can change a game.

MIKE CHANNON

So often the pendulum continues to swing with the side that has just pulled themselves out of a hole.

TONY GUBBA

Numero Eins – as they say in Germany . . .

PETER JONES

Our fans have been branded with the same brush.

RON ATKINSON

Ian Rush unleashed his left foot and it hit the back of the net.

MIKE ENGLAND

You'll be hoping that this run of injuries will stop earlier than it started.

ANDREW GIDLEY

Ian Durant has grown both physically and metaphorically in the close season.

JOCK WALLACE

It will be a shame if either side lose. And that applies to both sides.

JOCK BROWN

At the end of the day, the Arsenal fans demand that we put eleven players on the pitch.

DON HOWE

Peter Shilton conceding five – you don't get many of that to the dozen.

DESMOND LYNAM

It's Great Britain in the all-white strip, with the red and blue V, the dark shorts and the dark stockings.

RAY FRENCH

Well Kerry, you're 19 and you're a lot older than a lot of people younger than yourself.

MIKE GRAY

United have a very experienced bench which they
may want to play to turn the tide of the match.

BRYON BUTLER

It was a good match which could have gone either way
and very nearly did.

JIM SHERWIN

Oh, he had an eternity to play that ball . . . but he took
too long over it.

MARTIN TYLER

Everything in our favour was against us.

DANNY BLANCHFLOWER

And so now the fair, long hair of Adrian Heath has been thrown into action.

BRYON BUTLER

I think everyone in the stadium went home happy, except all those people in Rumania.

RON GREENWOOD

Well, he had two stabs at the cherry.

ALAN GREEN

Butcher goes forward as Ipswich throw their last trump card into the fire.

BRYON BUTLER

Once again it was Gough who stood firm for Scotland in the air.

JOCK BROWN

The scoreline really didn't reflect the outcome.

TONY GUBBA

I can't promise anything but I can promise 100%.

PAUL POWER

John Lyall – very much a claret and blue man, from his stocking feet to his hair.

PETER JONES

Walsall have given City more than one anxious moment amongst many anxious moments.

DENIS LAW

Billy Gilbert hit a kamikaze back pass which Justin
Fashinu pounced on like a black Frank Bruno.

IAN DARK

Peter Weir has just shrugged off an ankle injury.

JOCK BROWN

Mark Ward has only got size 5 boots but he sure packs a hell of a punch with them.

BRIAN MOORE

McCarthy shakes his head in agreement with the referee.

MARTIN TYLER

Souness' football brain working at a hundred miles an hour out there.

BRIAN MOORE

Stevens got to the line, crossed the ball and Liniker
wrapped it all up with his head.

RALPH DELLOR

I'm afraid that Francis this season has been suffering
from a panacea of injury.

DALE BARNES

Manchester United are looking to Frank Stapleton to pull some magic out of the fire.

JIMMY HILL

It really needed the blink of an eyelid, otherwise you would have missed it.

PETER JONES

We've got nothing to lose, and there's no point losing this game.

BOBBY ROBSON

Northern Ireland were in white, which was quite appropriate because three inches of snow had to be cleared from the pitch before kick-off.

JOHN MOTSON

. . . and Bailey comes out to save; immediately, there is a whole wasps' nest of blue shirts swarming around him . . .

BRYON BUTLER

A win tonight is the minimum City must achieve.

ALAN PARRY

Golf

There he stands with his legs akimbo.

PETER ALLISS

Sandy Lyle talking to Tony Adamson – a lifelong ambition fulfilled.

IAN ROBERTSON

And now to hole eight which is in fact, the eighth hole.

PETER ALLISS

This is the twelfth – the green is like a plateau with the top shaved off.

RENTON LAIDLAW

He used to be fairly indecisive, but now he's not so certain.

PETER ALLISS

Hockey

Great Britain have turned upside down the pages of
world hockey history.

NIGEL STARMER-SMITH

Horse Racing

BROUGH SCOTT: 'What are your immediate
thoughts, Walter?'
WALTER SWINBURN: 'I don't have any
immediate thoughts at the moment.'

Steve Cauthen, well on his way to that mythical 200
mark.

JIMMY LINDLEY

A racing horse is not like a machine. It has to be tuned
up just like you tune up a racing motor car.

CHRIS POOL

These two horses have met five times this season, and
I think they've beaten each other on each occasion.

JIMMY LINDLEY

Motor Racing

Speaking from memory, I don't know how many
points Nelson Piquet has got . . .

MURRAY WALKER

Thackwell really can metaphorically coast home now.

MURRAY WALKER

And all Niki really has to do now is coast,
metaphorically speaking.

MURRAY WALKER

Alain Prost is in a commanding second position.

MURRAY WALKER

A mediocre season for Nelson Piquet as he is now known and always has been.

MURRAY WALKER

With two laps to go then the action will begin, unless this is the action, which it is . . .

MURRAY WALKER

There are four different cars filling the first four places.

MURRAY WALKER

And now Jacques Laffitte is as close to Surer as Surer is to Laffitte.

MURRAY WALKER

Brundle is driving an absolutely pluperfect race.

MURRAY WALKER

Nigel Mansell is the last person in the race apart from the five in front of him.

MURRAY WALKER

Oddballs

You have to be Grace Darling – go out on your horse and rescue drowning people.

GERMAINE GREER

No programme about Venice would be complete without an Italian tenor, and here he is to sing 'Mama', Wynford Evans.

TED ROGERS

Time, as they say, is the essence of all evil.

JIM SYMON

There are no winners and no losers. Everybody loses.

IAN MacGREGOR

Here are the two men who now have a major headache on their hands.

RICHARD WHITELEY

I believe if there's coal in the ground, it's better to get it out now than leave it to rot forever.

BILL SURDS

We don't want to see these coal fields trampled into
the ground.

RODNEY BICKERSTAFFE

I would have thought that whichever way you slice the
cake, the government has certainly got itself into an
almighty pickle.

JIMMY YOUNG

There they all are, like ants, beavering away.
SIR JOHN H. PLUMB

The timber in the roof was completely comprised of wood.

STANLEY PHILLIPS
(*N. Yorks Fire Officer*)

The TUC will have a major headache on its hands . . .
NICHOLAS JONES

I'd tell you about my weekend but I can't remember much about it. Spent my birthday in Paris. Unforgettable experience.

PETER POWELL

You could count them on less than one hand.
MOTORCYCLISTS' ASSOCIATION SPOKESMAN

TED ROGERS: 'You're a part-time care assistant?'
CONTESTANT: 'Yes'
TED ROGERS: 'Is that a full-time job or part-time?

Did you find yourself reminiscing a great deal in your autobiography?

GLORIA HUNNIFORD

Sixteen minutes past nine is the time – a little earlier than usual.

DOUGLAS CAMERON

Who wrote the 1812 Overture? (*On receiving the answer 'Beethoven'.*) That's an educated guess.

JIM BOWEN

It's impossible to predict how he (Arthur Scargill) will react when he keeps saying the same things over and over again.

JOHN EGAN

I needed a break from the programme in order to regurgitate myself.

FRED FEAST

We haven't demanded anything. What we have demanded is that the coal board withdraw their demands.

ARTHUR SCARGILL

Dudley Moore without a piano is like chalk without cheese.

NICK OWEN

We shall have no coal industry if the miners are driven into the ground.

CLAIRE BROOKS

But if his anger shows now, it'll soon evaporate into a real question mark.

SIMON REED

Not many people realise just how well-known he is.

LORD GOWRIE

A concrete pipe reduced to mere matchwood.

PETER McCANN

In Nuremburg the ubiquitous smell of sausages
seems to be everywhere.

FRANCES DONNELLY

Mrs Maggie Backhouse – looking calm but tense at
the end of her husband's trial.

RICHARD EVANS

You're a fourth generation chef. What did your
father do.

LUCIEN FREUD

She has won three thousand pounds already, in as
many years.

DEBBIE THROWER

Today is the 40th anniversary of the RAF bombing
Dresden. That was during the war.

SIMON BATES

. . . and a shame that anybody who didn't turn up
wasn't there.

TONY BLACKBURN

He smokes like a fish.

SIMON BATES

A couple of months ago few had ever heard of AIDS.
Now everyone knows about it. Some of us even know
that it stands for Acquired Immune Deficiency
Disease.

BARBARA MYERS

An urgent traffic report: there has been an accident
on the Severn Bridge. Between England and Wales.

IAN DARK

The government will have to reap a very severe
whirlwind in the shape of a backlash from the public.

RODNEY BICKERSTAFFE

Treat them like children, and that means giving them
plenty of nitrogen fertiliser . . .

GEOFFREY SMITH

MAX BYGRAVES: 'And what do you do?'
CONTESTANT: I'm a housewife and mother.'
MAX BYGRAVES: 'Do you have any children?'

If daggers are not actually drawn they are certainly
out of their sheaths.

PAUL ROSS

THE WELSH PAINTER DAVID HOCKNEY

. . . the French painters of that time, Picasso for instance . . .

DAVID HOCKNEY

Elizabeth Taylor was a far bigger woman than Richard Burton.

PENNY JUNOR

No one's predicting the outcome (of the appeal) but, judging by historic precedent, it could go either way.

ROBIN GOULD

It's like the War of the Roses all over again. We have one Scottish contestant and one English contestant.

SIMON BATES

While he was in intensive care she was carrying a baby that wasn't hers.

TONY BLACKBURN

Of the designs of mine that succeed, 50% of them don't.

ZANDRA RHODES

A lot of people think the hard noses of Fleet Street
don't have a soft centre, but they do you know.

GERALD WILLIAMS

The problem with heart disease is that the first
symptom is often sudden death, and that's a very hard
symptom to deal with . . .

DR MICHAEL PHELPS

. . . they are inviting their colleagues to march down a
cul-de-sac which has no end.

PETER SMITH

You do not unilaterally change horses in mid-stream.
RON TODD

We've done this in many African countries – Nigeria,
Sierra Leone, Trinidad.

PETER LESLIE

You have reached a turning point on a voyage of no
return.

SIMON BATES

At this moment there is not a problem at this
moment.

DAVID PLEAT

The 'phone is going like a Christmas tree.

SIMON BATES

Then at the back we have a holster for a revolver –
that in itself opens another can of beans.

MICHAEL YARDLEY

Far be it from me to say that New Zealand is a racist
country but, yes, New Zealand is a racist country.

KERI HULME

It's now just coming up to eight minutes to two, that's
the time of course.

BRUNO BROOKS

It's nine minutes past three, timewise of course.
PAUL JORDAN

The pendulum has gone full circle.
JIMMY YOUNG

We flew straight up; 4,000 feet in as many minutes!

RADIO ONE

But surely, by demystifying Macbeth, you're taking the mystery out of it.

BARRY NORMAN

And the time left in clock terms is about five minutes.

ARCHIE McPHERSON

And that's what happens when two immovable objects meet.

RAY FRENCH

We don't stand behind our wives like some miners; our wives are in front of us.

YORKSHIRE MINER

See you at the same time next week, at the brand new time of 4.20.

PRESENTER, TYNE TEES TV

I think it's a good thing because most people haven't got time on weekdays to do any Sunday shopping.

PEBBLE MILL AT ONE

And did you see Silas Marner last night? That Ben Kingsley didn't look one bit like Gandhi. Fantastic!

SIMON BATES

And that's a self-portrait of himself, by himself.

RICHARD MADELEY

The media gave us the rough end of the wedge.

JOHN TAYLOR

I have been assaulted more times than I can count; about four or five times.

YOU AND YOURS

It all depends on whether there are any more hot potatoes waiting to come over the horizon.

WILLIAM MADEL M.P.

And when Neil Kinnock speaks tonight, he'll be speaking in an area where the working miners evenly outnumber those on strike.

SUSANNAH SIMONS

You can't, in five minutes, transfer sovereignty overnight.

MAX HASTINGS

Politics

I was stunned with outrage . . .

NEIL KINNOCK

That's my gut standing and that's where I stand.

DAVID PENHALIGON

He can talk over the heads of the intelligentsia to grass roots level.

JOHN BROWN M.P.

Britain was still a very great power in 1948–9–10.

SHIRLEY WILLIAMS

In the Upper House, their Lordships carry on regardless, TV cameras blazing.

BRIAN SHALLCROSS

In that tense situation people get tense.

ERIC HEFFER

We are sitting on a powder-keg that could explode in our faces at any time.

BISHOP TUTU

This Bill enables the Secretary of State to plunge into the waters of local government, with his head firmly buried in the sand.

BARONESS BURKE

He and his colleagues are like hungry hounds
galloping after a red herring.

WILLIAM SHELTON M.P.

The Home Secretary has nailed his flag to the wall.

DON CONCANNON M.P.

I would expect things to go on much as they are, until
there is some change.

SIR ANTHONY PARSONS

What we're not going to do is set down an ideology on tablets of stone and wave it in the air.

                    IAN WRIGGLESWORTH M.P.

The people doing these murders are masquerading openly in the streets.

                    IAN PAISLEY M.P.

That NUPE candidate should put her voice where her mouth is.

DEREK HATTON

There are more crimes in Britain now, due to the huge rise in the crime rate.

NEIL KINNOCK

We're a year nearer the general election than we were this time last year.

JOHN COLE

If people had proper locks on their doors, crime could be prevented before it happens.

DOUGLAS HURD

Pop

If Shaking Stevens were to retire, this man could well become his predecessor.

PETE SMITH

Thank you for all the entries in the Abba competition. There were 30,000 entries, so you stand a one in a million chance of winning one of the ten prizes.

SIMON BATES

That's one of those songs that's going to go on and on and be popular even when people forget about it.

STEVE COLLINS

Two of the great song-writing teams there . . . Lennon and McCartney and Ivor Novello . . .

JIMMY SAVILE

And there he was, reigning supreme at number two.

ALAN FREEMAN

Also in the news, the case of Rudolph Hess, the guy who's in Spandau Ballet . . .

SIMON BATES

And that was CCS Society – so much easier to pronounce than say.

DAVID (KID) JENSEN

That guitarist is almost going back to The Beatles' 'She's a Woman' days. Good stuff. Highly original.

DAVE LEE TRAVIS

Anybody buying the record can be assured that the pound they pay will literally go into someone's mouth.

BOB GELDOF

This was a big hit; it was in the top ten and got to number 15.

DAVID HAMILTON

You've had a lot of hits under the bridge since then.

WALLY WHYTON

That was a reminder of an unforgettable voice.

JOHN STILES

Mike Oldfield named an album after a geographical area in Britain. Can you name either the area or the album?

PETER POWELL

I had written a few songs and asked Robert Palmer to write the words and tunes.

ANDY TAYLOR (DURAN DURAN)

Managing the Beatles was another bow to Brian Epstein's string.

PETE BEST

This was the year we lost Sir Ralph Richardson, and gained THIS from Kajagoogoo.

SIMON BATES

What a simple tune. It's a wonder nobody thought of it first.

STEVE RACE

It's been every colour under the rainbow.

TOYAH WILCOX

PAUL KING: In Italy they call me the Pink Panther. Don't ask me why.
SIMON BATES: Why do they call you that?

Rugby

It shows what a hot seat that number 9 jersey has been.

NIGEL STARMER-SMITH

Paul Allott drying the wet ball which is a disadvantage in Lancashire's favour.

FRANK HAYES

You have to be fairly one-dimensioned when the crunch comes down.

AUSTRALIAN RUGBY COACH

I don't want to sit on the fence but it could go either way.

MAURICE BANFORD

The Wigan defence allowed him two bites at the shot.

RADIO MANCHESTER REPORTER

A pressure kick for Andrew with Brown breathing down his throat.

NIGEL STARMER-SMITH

That could have made it 10–3, and there's a subtle difference between that and 7–3.

BILL MACLAREN

He's like a needle in a haystack, this man – he's everywhere!

RAY FRENCH

Sailing

There isn't a record in existence that hasn't been broken.

CHAY BLYTH

Snooker

Can Bill Werbenuik be the second Canadian to rewrite the history books?

TED LOWE

This young man Jimmy White celebrated his 22nd birthday literally four days ago.

TED LOWE

I like playing in Sheffield . . . it's full of melancholy happy-go-lucky people.

ALEX HIGGINS

John Spencer can't really afford to go 5–1 down at such an early stage.

JACK KARNEHAM

Alex, unlike many other professionals, adds a bit on his cue rather than put on an extension.

TED LOWE

And Griffiths has looked at that blue four times now, and it still hasn't moved.

TED LOWE

After 12 frames, they stand all square. The next frame, believe it or not, is the 13th.

DAVID VINE

But there was still the big prize money – hanging there like a carrot waiting to be picked.

DAVID VINE

He's 40 points behind and there's only 51 points left on the table.

TED LOWE

That cue arm, now in perfect rhythm with his thinking . . .

JOHN PULLMAN

He has to stay level, or one frame behind, that's the only way he can beat him.

DENNIS TAYLOR

That's inches away from being millimetre perfect.

TED LOWE

Well it seems at the moment as if the pockets are as big as goal posts for Willie Thorne.

JOHN PULLMAN

The formalities are now over and it's down to
business; Steve Davis now adjusting his socks.
                                    TED LOWE

Steve, with his sip of water, part of his make-up.
                                    TED LOWE

Well, the shot would have been safe if the red hadn't
ended up over the pocket.
                                    TED LOWE

Steve Davis is trailing by one frame, so the pressure is balanced on him.

REX HARRIS

He's obviously worked out for himself that he doesn't need that last red . . . great thinker this man.

DENNIS TAYLOR

And Jimmy's potting literally doing the commentary here.

TED LOWE

He's completely disappeared. He's gone back to his dressing room. Nobody knows where he has gone.

TED LOWE

We do still get letters about 'kicks', there's no explanation – it's a little piece of dirt on the cue-ball.

DENNIS TAYLOR

Swimming

If our swimmers want to win any more medals, they'll have to put their skates on.

DAVE BRENNER

Tennis

Chris Lloyd came out of the dressing room like a pistol.

VIRGINIA WADE

Strangely enough, Kathy Jordan is getting to the net first, which she always does.

FRED PERRY

Ann's got to take her nerve by the horns.

VIRGINIA WADE

Lloyd did what he achieved with that shot.

JACK BANNISTER

Diane – keeping her head beautifully on her shoulders.

ANN JONES

That shot he's got to obliterate from his mind a little bit.

MARK COX

And here's Zivojinovic, six foot six inches tall and
fourteen pounds ten ounces.

DAN MASKELL

. . . Zivojinovic seems to be able to pull the big bullet
out of the top drawer.

MIKE INGHAM

If she gets the jitters now, then she isn't the great
champion that she is.

MAX ROBERTSON

He (McEnroe) has got to sit down and work out where he stands.

FRED PERRY

Martina, she's got several layers of steel out there like a cat with nine lives.

VIRGINIA WADE

Chip Hooper is such a big man that it is sometimes difficult to see where he is on the court.

MARK COX

Those two volleys; really could be the story of this match summed up at the end of it.

BARRY DAVIES

PRIVATE EYE

We're giving nothing away!

It's only

£10

And read Colemanballs every fortnight

for one year's subscription

It's so quick and easy; just fill in and send us the form below and we will start sending you Private Eye from the next issue.

- ✂

To PRIVATE EYE SUBSCRIPTIONS, Mortimer House, 230 Lavender Hill, London SW11

Please send me PRIVATE EYE for the next year (12 months). I enclose £10.00 (cheques, P.O.s payable to Private Eye)

NAME ....

ADDRESS ....

....